The Derners
A Play by Mary Strathie

For my big brothers Adam and Ronnie and my big sis Betty for such a happy childhood and treating me like a wee princess.

Acknowledgement

My first thanks must go to the Dramateurs for being so brave to put on an unknown play by an amateur writer's first effort. Also to Paul Johnston who made my sketchy effort at lyric writing into workable songs and writing the lovely music to accompany them. Thanks also to Derek Calder who arranged the music and played at all dramateurs performances.

I must also say a big thank you to by dear friend Muriel Johnston whose help in too many ways to list was invaluable. Last but by no means least my thanks to Deborah Howden for her patience in deciphering my atrocious writing and spelling, for typing this out for me and also the original play script.

A Dream Come True

In February 1993, two months after our first production of 'The Derners', by public demand the Dramateurs decided to do another three nights. It was a chancy thing to do. Would we really sell enough tickets again to cover our costs? We needn't have worried. The tickets had gone a week before the performances so with demands for tickets still being made, we turned our dress rehearsal into a performance, selling tickets at the door. Nearly two hundred were sold.

At one of the performances in this run we were being judged for the 'Muriel Ovens Quaich', a trophy for amateur players in the Borders. The adjudicator for this was Anne Plenderleith, Director of Rideout Theatre. She gave us a very favourable adjudication and 'The Dramateurs' won the Quaich. A few weeks later Anne approached me and asked if she could put on 'The Derners' professionally. Needless to say I was over the moon. It took a lot of hard work and many months for Anne and Rideout to raise enough finance to tour 'The Derners'. Rideout did sixteen performances in towns and villages all over the Borders and was successful everywhere.

I have many wonderful memories of this time. The thrill of hearing so many people laugh and then dab an eye, then laugh again was wonderful but one big kick I got was when Anne asked if I would be voice coach (teach them the Galashiels accent) for the professional actors as only one of the cast was from the Borders. Imagine, I was getting paid for something I used to get a clip round the ear for.

Dramateurs Cast

Cora:	Muriel Johnston
Jessie:	Nancy Bain
Jean:	Jan Duncanson
Lil:	Susan Dalgleish
Martha:	Lynn Allen
Rena:	Wendy McBain
Maisie:	Louise Howden
Mr Mack:	Donald McKelvie
Molly:	Catherine Bain
Sadie:	Mary Strathie
Director:	Morag Watson

Rideout Cast

Cora:	Chris Melville
Jessie:	Ruth Smith
Jean:	Hope Ross
Lil:	Nell Brennan
Martha:	Una Ailsa MacNab
Rena:	Helen Lomax
Maisie:	Maria Miller
Mr Mack:	Ian Briggs
Director:	Anne Plenderleith

Act One

1953 – The week before the Gala Day

Monday morning seven forty-five and as usual Cora is first in the darning flat, for the past forty years it had been so, she hates the rush in the fifteen minutes before eight o'clock when all the mill hooters blast across Galashiels and hundreds of workers rush in different directions to the many Tweed Mills in the town. Then suddenly at one minute past eight the town is silent, except as you pass the mills when the clank-clank of the looms can be heard from outside.

Cora is reading her daily paper as usual, when first to arrive is Jessie who is the motherly type, everyone knows you can tell your troubles to her, plus she will give good advice and your secret will go no further. 'Morning Cora, it's no a bad day is it'.

'Aye it's lovely Jessie. Did ye come doon Scott Street? Aw the flags are up it looks a fair treat'. 'Na a didnae see them, a came doon the long stairs'.

Jean comes bustling in and goes to her seat without speaking. She is in her forties and not the easiest person in the darning flat to get along with as she is a bit of a boast. She loves her possessions and is always the first to get any new gadgets and makes sure everyone knows how well off she is.

'Oor jist sayin it's a grand mornin Jean'.

'No afore time, a thought oo were never goin tae get ony summer' she snaps at Jessie. Cora, not wanting her to get away with snapping at Jessie 'Oh but Jean oo've had a lot o grand days, it's been a guid summer'.

'Well ave never noticed it'.

With that Lil breezes in. Jean and Lil have known each other since childhood and are old adversaries since teenage years but in a strange way are still friends and Lil likes nothing better than to rub Jean up the wrong way and get her on her high horse.

Lil is happy go lucky, always wears full make up and is always well dressed, bordering a little on tarty. 'What have ye no noticed Jean?, it's no like you tae

Galashiels Dramateurs, the original cast of the "The Derners".

On the lookout. Rideout Theatre Company in "The Derners" Tour 1994.

miss onything' and then to everyone else 'Morning all, great day isn't it'. 'It is that Lil' Jessie replies quickly before Jean can retaliate and start a fight.

'Oh Jessie a saw your young John at the Polish Club on Saturday night, he's gettin tae be a fine big handsome young man'. There's a real twinkle in Lil's eye as she says this and Jessie has to laugh

'You jist keep your eyes off him Lil, he's our young for ee'.

'Mair's the pity, if a had bin ten years younger mind you!'.

At this Jean gives a huge snort of disapproval 'Ten years! – whae are you kiddin – mair like twenty, an then some'.

As she says this the mill hooter blasts as Maisie and Rena tumble through the doors out of breath and panting. 'Jist made it by the skin o oor teeth' Maisie announces throwing herself down on her seat.

'Yin o these days Maisie oo'll be in first, a wid ay clocked Martha in hur Hitler was standin by the clock'.

Jean who hasn't much time for the younger ones' daftness begins to lecture the girls in her posh voice. 'If you mean Mr Mack say so, he is your boss after all and he is just doing his job. You young ones don't show enough respect for your elders'.

As she is laying down the law to Rena, Maisie is copying her behind her back, Jean sees the rest smiling and turns round almost in time to catch Maisie, but Maisie is too quick.

Maisie is sixteen and in her first year as apprentice darner. She hasn't a worry in the world, the youngest by a long way of five children and is loved and adored by all her family. She loves going to the pictures and spends four, if not five nights being transported to another world in the Pavilion or the Playhouse.

In her year as an apprentice she has learned how to humour Jean. 'Aw Jean dinnae be sae serious, it's the Gala week' as she gives her a hug. 'Lets hae some fun tae get us in the mood. I'll bet you bought something nice this weekend, are you gaun tae tell us what it was?'

This is just the opportunity Jean has been waiting for and a bright smile spreads over her face, this gets everyone's attention as this doesn't happen very often. She, knowing this was her moment of triumph, was really going to make them envious and she started slowly 'Well . . . as a matter of fact . . . I bought a Television Set!'

It had the desired effect, everyone spoke at once. 'Well I never' was Jessie's reaction, 'that takes the bloody biscuit' was Lils, and Cora who wasn't too up on modern technology chipped in 'is that when ee get pictures on yer wireless?' Rena was delighted for her 'that's smashing Jean' and Maisie, who couldn't think of anything more wonderful than seeing all the stars at the flick of a switch in your own home declared 'Oh Jean, Jean if ee ever get a musical on can a come an see it?'

Jean savoured her moment, it was better than she expected and very grandly announced 'I'll have ee aw roond some night. It's really guid, naebody went oot the whole weekend, no even ma James, he's no missed a Saturday night at the Auld Mill for long enough. Twae o' his pals came up on Sunday tae see if he was no weel'.

They are all laughing at this as Martha comes in looking very subdued. She is twenty three but looks older, a bit old fashioned looking but a very nice girl. She comes from Huddersfield and has been working in Galashiels for about a year, she has nearly finished her apprenticeship. 'Hello everybody'.

'Hello Martha'. Jessie always worries if there's something wrong with the young ones. 'Yer late hen (Martha gives a startled look) did ee sleep in?'

Presentation to Braw Lad and Lass and Attendant, 1961 at Comelybank Mill.

Comelybank Mill staff model the latest hair-do's.

Maisie still excited about the news 'Fancy Martha, Jean's got a television set'. Martha looks impressed.

Lil can contain herself no longer. 'You'll be wantin an inside lavvy next Jean, so nane o' ye need tae leave the hoose at aw'. This remark has exactly the effect she was hoping for.

Jean bristles, straightens her back and puts on her best 'Morningside' accent. 'You always have to lower the tone Lil, don't you? But as soon as our Linda gets married, we'll have room to pit a lavvy (corrects herself) put a bathroom in, so there.'

Jessie, trying to change the subject quickly and keep the peace asks everybody 'Well did awbody hae a guid weekend? You first Cora, what did you get up to?' All the darners are now busy at work, the younger ones sitting with an older one so she can learn as she works.

'Well!!' Cora begins as if she is about to tell them about a very exciting weekend, 'a went tae the whist on Friday night at the Y.M.C.A. but a didnae win. Mrs Newlands won, she's a grand player, she often wins'.

'On Saturday a had a look roond the shops and a picked up a new skirt a was haein made at Currie McDougall and Scotts. Oh it wis awfae nice, they make a grand job'. As she is telling her story Maisie and Rena are looking at each other and giggling at the fact that Cora considers this so exciting, Jean gives Rena a hefty dig in the ribs as Cora continues. 'At night a listened tae the wireless and on Sunday a had ma tea wie ma sister an ma niece. It was a grand weekend, a fair enjoyed masel'.

Adam Renton, the author's dad, busy at work. 1955.

Lil pipes in immediately with 'a dinnae think a can top that for excitement Cora, but I'll try'. Giggles from the girls and a sneer from Jean.

'On Friday night, Peter and masel went tae the Auld Time Dancin, only they dinnae call it that now – it's Sequence Dancin, awbody daein the same step at the same time. Aggie and Adam Renton are the teachers. There were aboot eighty folk there, it's really guid. You wid fair enjoy it Jessie'. She wanders over to Jean and very pointedly says 'You tae Jean – your Dave wis an awfie guid dancer if a mind right'. Again she makes Jean bristle as she meant her too.

Laughing she goes on 'On Saturday we were at the Polish Club for a drink an a guid laugh', then she comes to the pièce de la resistance. 'On Sunday ma darling Peter and me walked up Meigle Hill an then, an then', she emphasises 'we went tae the Royal Hotel for a high tea'. There are ooh's and aah's from everyone at such a treat.

Jessie, keeping control as usual on the weekend goings-on invites the young ones to tell their story. 'So what aboot you young yins now, were ee at the dancin?, Martha what aboot you? Hey Martha!' Martha is miles away. 'Hey Martha!'.

'Oh sorry Jessie I didn't hear you. No I didn't have a very exciting weekend. My aunt and uncle were up from Huddersfield. He's looking for a job up here in a spinning department, the same as my dad'.

'Well there's plenty o jobs gaun for guid workers' says Lil.

Martha nods and looking very fed up goes on. ' The conversation was about cloth, mills and spinning all day Saturday, and on Sunday we were all at church twice'.

Jessie trying to cheer Martha up 'Mind you, a think they sing awfae happy hymns at the Baptist Church'.

Martha gives her a little smile of gratitude, 'Later, I wrote a letter to Ian, and that was my weekend'.

Maisie trying to brighten the conversation starts to tell them about, what was for her, a very exciting weekend. 'A had a super duper weekend, a was at the Pin on Friday night and saw a smashin Doris Day picture, a saw it on Tuesday an aw. Jimmy Smith says am yin o' their best customers, but he never offers me a discount'. As she is working she starts to sing to

Phillis Calvert visits Pringles of Hawick.

The darning flat, Gardiners Mill, Selkirk. circa 1948.

herself, Secret Love, when she stops there's a round of applause and comments on her nice voice, she is a little embarrassed.

Cora suggests she should be on the stage.

'Oh a wish a could be Cora. On Saturday a got a right surprise, ye ken it's ma birthday on the Gala Day, well ma mum and dad an ma brothers and sister aw pit the gether and geen me the money tae buy a Dansette'.

Cora looks very bewildered. 'What on earth's that hen?'

'It's a record player Cora'.

Jessie, very impressed says 'that's lovely hen, they're quite dear are they no?'

Jean again jumping in with a chance to boast 'we gave our Linda a very expensive one for her birthday'.

Nobody takes any notice of her, and Maisie continues with her story. 'A didnae expect tae get one. I've only been naggin for twae months, it usually takes much longer than that'.

Rena smiles at Maisie and without malice says 'your spoilt Maisie, yer a lucky thing'. Rena doesn't know what it's like to be spoilt or coddled. She is the youngest of a family of five and since her mother died when she was fourteen has had to be cook, housekeeper and general dogsbody to her father and four older brothers. She is not jealous of Maisie, only pleased that she has such a nice life.

'A ken am lucky Rena, well me an ma mum went tae Coull's and bought one, it's blue, an a got twae records, a Judy Garland and a Guy Mitchell'. She breaks into song, 'she wears red feathers and a hula hula skirt', everybody joins in and Cora gets up from her table and does her version of a hula dance to everyone's amusement. They all have a laugh as they finish.

Jean, never one to miss an opportunity 'My Linda has about thirty records now', again nobody takes notice and Maisie continues 'A jist keep playin them ower and ower again. A think they're wishin they hadnae got it for me awready. At night a went tae the Palais, and listen tae this, a got a set hame'

'Isn't that nice' says Cora, 'Yer a bit young for that' says Jean. 'Was he nice, div oo' ken him?' says Jessie. Rena asks 'Was it that fella that was dancin wie ye at the end?'.

'Aye it was Rena, his name was Jim an he came frae Selkirk'.

All give a mock groan and say together in horror 'Frae Selkirk!' Cora, in a serious voice says 'Well he cannae help that puir laddie'.

Many hours were spent here learning our trade. Netherdale Mill, Galashiels. circa 1950.

Photo-call at Pringles Mill, Hawick.

'A dinnae think I'll see him again though'. Rena is surprised at this 'What for no, he looked really nice'. 'Oh aye Rena he looked nice enough but he was a bit fresh'.

Lil, always wanting to know the juicy bits 'Do tell us more'.

'Well ee ken what they're like Lil'. Lil gives her a knowing look. 'His hands were everywhere, you know whit a mean, a kept pushing them away. Efter a wee while he stood back, hands on his hips, an says what's wrong, have ye no got ony'.

At this they all laugh, 'the thing is Lil, maybe he was right'. 'What dae ye mean Maisie?' Giggling Maisie replies 'Well Lil, if a had some a might o let him'.

All go 'Ooo Ooo'. Cora not quite sure what she means says 'Yer an awfae lassie Maisie'.

They all resume their work but Jessie is worried about Martha's quiet mood. 'Martha! You've hardly said a word aw mornin'. Cora had noticed too, 'aye Martha ee look like somebody's stolen yer scone, are ee aw right hen?'

'I've just got something on me mind that's all'. 'Are ee missin Ian hen?' Jessie asks, wanting to get to the bottom of her problem. 'Yes, I am that

Jessie, it'll be another five weeks before he's home. I worry that he'll be sent to Korea.'

Maisie trying to cheer her friend up tells her 'No much fear o that Martha. At the pictures on Friday night on the Pathe News, they said it wid be aw ower in a few months so dinnae worry'.

Cora gives this a little thought then states 'Aye an they said the 1st World War was the war to end all wars, they didnae ken what they were talkin aboot – did they? They were just talkin through a hole in their mooth.' They all smile knowingly at each other, just another of Cora's miss-quotes. But Martha is still upset and shocks everyone with her next statement

'Bloody National Service!!!'

Jessie not believing her ears 'Martha – ave never heard ye swear afore.' Martha close to tears dashes out of the flat saying 'Its just spoiling oor lives.' 'Puir lass a thought there was somethin wrong wi her this mornin,'

'Aye Jessie it's rotten for them engaged and sae much in love. A mind what its like – ee just want tae be the gether aw the time, a still dinnae like being away frae ma Peter.'

Braemar Mill, Hawick badminton team, 1950's.

'Aye, puir lass, still as the saying goes'. They are all alert for another of Cora's wonderful sayings 'Every sky has a blue lining'. She didn't let them down.

Jessie still concerned 'I'll hae a wee word wie her when she comes back'.

Rena wanting to help 'Will a go tae the lav an see if she's aw right Jess'. 'Na hen a think she needs a wee bit time tae hersell, well then where were oo, oh aye, catchin up on the weekend. Jean yours must hae been gie excitin gettin a television set, tell us aw aboot it'.

Jean brightens up immediately, doesn't need coaxing, and is happy to share her good fortune with them all 'A think a had jist aboot the best weekend ave ever had in a long time. On Friday night oo had a family meetin tae discuss the buyin o the television set, cos oo couldnae get it if oo hadnae aw been pitten the gether. They're awfie, awfie dear ee ken, an oor three lads and twae lassies are aw in guid jobs, plus Dave and mysell. So oo aw agreed tae get yin on Saturday. Yince they had aw cleared oot, a thought a'd better dae ma cleanin cos a widnae get a chance the rest o the weekend, watchin the television ee ken. Well a hadnae cleaned oot ma china cabinet for ages'.

At this stage the others are all giving each other sly looks and smiles as they know what's coming, except for Cora who is listening with fascination about all Jean's grand things.

Jean continues, 'A washed aw ma best china an ma crystal and then did aw ma ornaments. As a was fair in a cleanin mood a polished aw the surroonds afore cleanin the kitchen cabinet. Did a tell ee a got a kitchen cabinet a few weeks ago? (everyone nods) By that time a wis fair jiggered so, as a had the hoose tae masel, a jist had a guid wash doon in front o the fire and then went tae ma bed.

Everyone sighs with relief thinking she has finished, when.

'Well in the mornin a couldnae believe it, Dave brought me ma breakfast in bed, was that no guid o him?'

Lil, not being able to resist says 'One o life's true gentlemen, a bet he even takes the dishes oot o the sink afore he has a pee'. Jean is furious 'Do you want tae hear or no?'

Jessie trying to keep the peace 'yes Jean, yes' and looking very pointedly at Lil 'Divn't oo?', 'Aye, aye, am aw bloody ears'.

Jean continues 'OK then. Well on Saturday mornin a had a hair appointment at Masion Emmas, a gaun every two weeks ee ken. When a came oot, a met Dave, Colin an James an oo went across tae the store for the television set. A picked yin like a cabinet, the doors shut up when yer no watchin it. The man said it'll be next week afore I can get you an aerial up. Quick as a flash oor James says, nae problem am a slater an ave pit up a few already so ool jist hae the lot away wie us. He aye has the works van, so tae cut a long story short (Lils eyes go up to the ceiling) it was aw fixed up by tea time and tae celebrate oo aw had steak for oor tea'. Cora's mouth falls open.

Lil moves over to Jean's table saying as she goes 'My, my, Jean have ee no come up in the world. Televisions, china cabinets and steak for tea, a can mind when yer breek erse wis hangin oot, an breed and drippin wis a guid day'.

Jean is really angry now, she stands up to face Lil, hands on her hips 'Ye cheeky bitch, an a can mind no as far back as that when their wasnao a Canadian sodger or a Pole in the toon that didnae have yer breeks roond yer ankles'. She clasps her hand over her mouth not believing she has said such

Learning the trade. Scottish Woollen Technical College, Netherdale Mills, Galashiels. circa 1950.

Mary Renton (Strathie) at work looking for a broken thread, 1955.

a thing. Everyone else is stunned and go back to work as if they hadn't heard.

Lil is very hurt as she just meant to have a bit of fun. 'A didnae mean what a said in a nasty way Jean, a jist meant, well mair o us were no sae weel off back then an you came frae an awfae big family, thirteen o ye in a gie wee hoose. Am no surprised yer prood o the lovely things and fine family ee've got. A ken you'll no believe it but am glad for ee. A ken you never liked me Jean, and why? Because your Dave and I went the gether afore he went oot wie you. A think oo were seventeen and it was only for a few weeks. It was a long time ago. A dinnae ken why ee always seem sae discontented and sae pleased tae hear o other folks misfortune. Ee seem tae hae a soor ploom in yer mooth aw the time. An as for what ee said aboot me Jean, a wasnae mairit, so a did hae a guid time, no as guid as you made oot mind ee. A did hae a lot o boyfriends and there were a lot o women jealous o that, so they made up stories, making me oot tae be a lot worse than a was. Once a met ma Peter a never looked at another man again (she saunters away then takes in everybody else) well no seriously onyway'.

Mary Curran (Dickie) training at the college – "Greasy Darning". 1952.

Mary Dickie (Curran). Still darning in the 1980's at Bernat Klein's.

Jessie, ever the peace maker, tries to put things right 'Am shair Jean didnae mean what she said Lil, did ye Jean?'

Cora putting her tuppenceworth in says 'Well ee ken what they say. He who throws sticks should live in a greenhoose'. They all laugh and this eases the tension somewhat.

Jean looking a bit ashamed 'Yer maybe right Lil, a was jealous but every time a ask Dave, were you his first .. ee ken, he wid jist smile and say 'a gentlemen doesn't tell'.

'A gentlemen doesn't tell', replies Lil, 'well am tellin ye now, if Dave had a first afore you it wasnae me, and that's the truth'. Jean gives a sigh of relief and a small smile. 'Am glad tae ken that after aw thae years Lil, maybe a can spit that soor ploom oot now'. 'That's guid Jean an while yer at it, maybe ye'll gie us a rest frae hearin everyday aboot aw the fine things ye have'.

Braemar Mill, Hockey Team, 1950's.

THINGS

Things why do they mean so much to me
was it that when I was wee
I never had something that belonged to me
Things what is this desire in me
for buying every dress I see
is it because that as a lass
no frock was ever new to me

Things now that I'm a wife and mum
and I've got a tidy sum
I've put behind out of my mind
the shame of needing charity
Things they say the best in life are free
it didn't seem like that to me
now I am free from poverty
but things still mean so much to me

Jessie picks up the conversation 'Are ee aw gawn tae Lindean the night, its sic a nice ceremony.' 'What time dae the buses leave?' Maisie asks, 'aboot half past six a think' replies Rena. 'Am jist gaun tae watch the horses leave', 'quite right Cora, it looks like they'll hae a grand night for it. Am jist gaun tae see the horses off anaw, cos David Nixon's on the television set wi a grand magic show at half past seven, an a wid like tae see it'.

Again Jean has supplied Lil with bullets 'Its a guid job awbody's no got a television set or there'd be naebody at bloody Lindean at aw'.

Jessie interrupts quickly 'a dinnae think there's as much interest in aw the Gala Day events as there used tae be, it's a pity'. Maisie picks up on that topic 'ma Mum was jist sayin the same thing the other night Jessie, she was sayin in the early years, when they lived in Queen Street, they had a piano oot in the street an they were aw dancin and singin and they aw had tables wi food and drink and they danced and danced tae the early mornin.

Clean darning flat,
Heather Mills, Selkirk.

Busy at work.
Glebe Mill, Hawick.

'Aye' says Lil wistfully, 'there were some grand pairties then, an neebers were neebers in thae days'.

'An she was tellin me aboot ma christenin pairty and how, at the end, when they were takin back aw the stuff they had borrowed, chairs tae yin, cups an saucers tae another, knives and forks tae somebody else, ma Dad sat doon fair exhausted and said 'I'll no be surprised if Charlie Whitehead the painter disnae come in the now an take the bloody paper off the wa'.

As they are all laughing Molly, a young weaver, pops her head round the door. 'Hi Rena, are ee comin for a fag, ave got some patter'. As it's near tea break Rena and Maisie pick up their bags and as they leave tell Jessie they're going for a smoke. Cora gets out her flask of tea and pours one out for Lil. Jean keeps working. Jessie thinks this might be a chance to have a word with Martha,

'Martha, come here a minute hen', 'yes Jessie what is it?'. 'Am no meanin tae be nosey hen, but is onythin botherin ee, ee ken it'll no gaun any further'. 'I know that Jessie, and I was hoping to have a word with you'.

She puts her head down and is wringing her hanky. 'It's about being late

Ordeal for the bride to be. Lochcarron Mill, Galashiels.

Jessie', 'Aye but it wisnae that late hen, only 10 minutes'. 'I don't mean that Jessie, I mean late'. She pauses and looks at Jessie, 'two weeks late'. Jessie is very sympathetic as Martha knew she would be 'aw a see, ye puir wee soul'. She gives her a hug.

'Oh Jessie I'm so ashamed, I don't know what to do'. 'Oh Martha, yer no the first and ye'll no be the last tae be in this predicament'. 'But you know what my Mum and Dad are like Jessie, they are such strong Baptists, they're at church three nights a week and twice on Sundays and being an only child, I'm all they've got. I've heard what they say about other girls this has happened to. My Mum pointed out very clearly to Ian when he gave me my engagement ring – 'that's an engagement ring Ian not a wedding ring and you remember that'.

'Twae weeks isnae very late Martha, ye might no be ye ken'. 'But what if I am?, 'Ye've been engaged twae years Martha, ye'll jist hae tae get married quicker than ye were plannin tae. When were ee gaun tae onywie?', 'In a years time'. 'Well ee cannae wait that long hen, och it's no right tae hae tae wait aw that time when yer sae much in love. An ye dinnae need tae feel ashamed, it's only natural when ye're no seein each other for such long spells tae be sae gled tae be the gether again'. 'Its been an awful burden, I feel better already just for telling you Jessie'.

At this the girls come back in giggling, and as they all resume work Rena tells them 'that Sadie's been in the smokey for fifteen minutes and Hitler had tae gaun an shout her oot. He said if she dis it again she'll get her cairds'.

Jean disapprovingly as ever she "say has tae over dae it that yin".

'Rena did ye enjoy the Palais on Saturday night' asks Jessie. 'Aye but a had an awfie big ironin tae dae first, they aw wanted a clean shirt for Saturday night'.

Lil is shocked at this 'It's no fair hen, a young lass like you, wi six grown men tae look efter. Dae nane o them help ee in the hoose?'.

'You must be kiddin Lil! Ma faither an ma brothers aw believe cookin and the hoose is woman's work. Am afraid ma mother, God rest her soul, spoilt them aw. She didnae gaun oot tae work, she was never very strong. When a hae a faimily, if a ever have a faimily, laddies and lasses will dae an equal share. The laddies will no be brought up tae think that hoosework is beneath them'. All nod in agreement. Maisie who knows what a hard life Rena has, is sympathetic.

'Nae wonder ee want tae emigrate tae America Rena', 'what does yer Dad think aboot ye gaun Rena?' asks Jean.

'Oh he just thinks its a norey, he disnae think I'll go. He widnae gie me permission, so a'll hae tae wait till am eighteen, roll on September then am off an they can all get on wie it their sels'. They all agree with her.

Cora has been giving this some thought and asks 'does it no cost an awfae lot o money Rena?', 'that's what ma faither thinks an aw, what he disnae ken is the family am gaun tae pays ma fare'.

Jean always looking on the black side 'a've heard that some o the lasses that go ower there are jist treated like skivvies'.

'Well a'd rather be a skivvy tae twae bairns than tae five ungrateful bloody men. Div ye ken what ma faither said to me on Sunday? A spent aw mornin makin a guid denner and he says 'a war awful disappointed when you were born a hooie Rena, I would have liked a fifth son, but it looks like ye've come in handy at last'.

They all can't believe such cruel words, Lil responds 'the ungrateful bugger!', Jessie 'that's awfie hen', Maisie shaking her head 'Nae wonder ye want oot o it Rena'.

Cora turns to Maisie 'Div ye no fancy gaun Maisie?', 'naw Cora, a'd miss ma faimily ower much'. With a smile Rena says 'but you've got a grand

"Off to a new life" — Farewell Party.

21

Elsa Darling gets her send-off from fellow workers Comelybank Mill, Galashiels.

faimily Maisie, they treat you like a wee princess'. 'A suppose it's cause am a lot younger than the rest o' them, div ye ken they still ca' me the bairn'.

'So did ye did eventually get tae the dancin' Rena', asks Jessie, 'Aye, but it was the back o' ten afore a got there an a was lucky cos Adam Crawford was on the door an he let me in for nothin'.

Cora has been thinking again, 'what kind o dancin' div thae dae nowadays, onyway?' Maisie, always ready for a bit fun and a skive says, 'come on Rena, let's show them. It's caud jivin' Cora'. As they jive they sing "Walking my Baby Back Home", the others join in the song and clap hands.

Cora is very impressed and Lil, always ready for a bit fun, walks over to Jean saying, 'It's no changed that much frae oor day. Oo did the jitterbug. Come on Jean oo'll show them'. Jean at first is reluctant and tells Lil, 'Dinnae be say daft', but Lil coaxes her and as she was a pretty good dancer in her day she can't resist to strut her stuff. They dance to "In the Mood" and they are good. Maisie and Rena can't believe this is the Jean they know.

There is lots of applause when they finish. Seeing the older ones dance has made Maisie think 'What about you Cora, how did you used tae dance'?

Lil says, 'It'll be the bloody minuet'. Cora gives Lil a dirty look. 'I'll show ye, just watch'. Cora does a wonderful Charleston and really surprises them and they hoop and cheer her on. At the end she is out of breath, gives a bit of a wobble and has to sit down.

After much laughter Jessie says 'Well oo'd better get back tae work'. They all settle back to work. Lil, always interested in what the young ones get up to, asks Rena, 'Did ee get a set hame frae the dancin' Rena'?

'As a matter o' fact, I did', says Rena, ' he was a nice fella, Bob Scott, he's a tuner at Comely Bank and he plays for Gala Rovers'. Maisie, wanting all the news, says, 'Are ee seein' him again Rena'? 'Aye am seein him on Torwoodlee night after the Braw Lads and Lasses Reel. He's takin' me tae Barries Chip Shop for a sit-in supper afore oo gaun tae the dancin'. Everyone oo's and ah's, Cora smiles at Rena.

'Oh that's grand Rena, ye'll no be calling the king yer uncle!', says Cora. Lil corrects her, 'cousin Cora' Cora looks bewildered and says, am no your cousin Lil'. Aw forget it Cora' says Lil.

Maisie, wanting to keep the conversation on the Braw Lads week, tells Rena, 'It's Tommy Graham on Wednesday night, he's aye guid but it's three

"Having a bit of fun". Rideout Theatre Company at Bowhill, 1994.

23

Gala's Braw Braw Lasses. Comelybank Mill darners.

Hawick's bright-eyed daughters at Braemar Ball.

shillin's instead o' half-a-croon'. Martha, who is trying to cheer up, says 'Are you all going to the dancing in the Scott Park on Friday night? Everybody says they probably will, Jessie tells them 'A like tae gaun for a wee while, then a like tae watch them gaun intae the ball an' see aw the lovely dresses'.

This makes Cora wonder, 'have ee aw got new frocks for the Gala Day then?' Maisie dying to tell somebody says 'Oh aye, only it's a no frock, it's a big wide skirt wie a lovely frilly petticoat and a button-up, 'am right pleased wie it. I'll be just like Alma Cogan'. Rena, really interested, says 'where did ye get it Maisie'? 'At Alex Mackays' says Maisie 'A've got a club there, have you got somethin' new Rena?', 'Aye, a got a nice frock at Leishmans'.

Lil asks Maisie ' what aboot that new shop that's just opened – Wilson's? They seem to have some lovely clathes in there'. 'Oh aye they have but ye cannae get tick in there'. Lil gasps, ' well a cannae see them selling much How aboot you Martha, have you got onything new'? 'No, because I'm saving up to get married, so I'm not bothering'.

The Bride gets a "send-off" from fellow workers. Comelybank Mill.

Mock Common Ridings within the mill. Hawick, late 1940's.

A look passes between Martha and Jessie. Rena, excited at news of a wedding, says ' Have ye set the date Martha?', 'No, but I don't want to wait as long as we were going to. I don't see the point'. Lil, with a leer, 'the urges gettin' too strong eh?' 'Oh, Lil you're awful so you are.'

Jean, thinking of the fun she could have planning a wedding 'when ma Linda gets mairrit' she's gaun tae hae a dress frae yin o they big shops in Edinburgh, maybe Jenners'. Nobody makes a comment but looks pass from one to another.

Maisie, imagining out loud again 'I'd like tae get mairrit in a frock just like Grace Kelly wore in . . .' Jean, not liking Maisie going one better ' dinnae rush too far aheid o yoursel, there's plenty time yet. Ye're no even gaun steady!' 'I dinnae mean I wanted tae get mairrit! I would just love a frock like that or maybe yin like Doris Day'.

Rena smiles indulgently at Maisie, she too has dreams. She turns to Martha and enquires 'have you decided what your gaun tae wear for your weddin, Martha?'

'Ever since I was a little girl I always wanted to get married in me grandma's wedding dress. Me mum wore it on her wedding day. When I got engaged, we got it out of it's box to see if it would fit, and fancy, the moths had been at it. I was so disappointed, it was so beautiful'.

'What a shame hen' says Jessie ' will it no mend'. 'No, it wer covered in holes. It was cream satin trimmed with Nottingham lace. I could cry when I think about it'. There's a brief, sad, silence while they think about the lovely dress.

Suddenly, Cora says ' ye could have mine, Martha!' Everybody stops work to look at each other, then at Cora, then at each other again. Has she finally flipped? Finally, Lil finds her voice and in a kind way, says 'but, but, ye've never mairrieed Cora'. Very chirpily Cora replies 'aye, a ken, but av'e aye been prepared – one of life's unclaimed jewels – that's me'.

Like Galashiels, other border towns, re-enacted a ceremony in the factory, prior to their festival.

"That's awfully kind of you Cora, I would love to see it', says Martha. There is a chorus of 'so wid a, and me an aw, oh! please bring it in Cora'. 'Well I'll bring it in some day this week and I'll maybe tell ye the story behind it'.

At this point Mr Mack (Hitler) the foreman walks in and tells Jessie 'A just thought ye'd like tae ken, Nellie Henderson jist got hit wie a shuttle. She's a pal o yours isn't she?' 'Oh no, is she hurt bad?' 'Well she's no too guid – it caught her on the heid'. 'Div ye think a should go up an see

Mock Common Ridings.

her?' 'Naw, naw they've tane her hame. A just thought ye'd like tae ken'. 'Thanks Mr Mack'.

He leaves as they all look a bit worried, thinking of poor Nellie. Cora cheers them up, 'A widnae be a weaver for aw' the coffee in China'. Rena corrects her 'tea Cora'. 'No thanks, hen, a just had yin'. Rena shrugs her shoulders and looks at the others as if to say, well I tried.

Lil remembers news of another weaver, 'did ye hear Kate Allen's leavin, Jessie'. 'Naw, is she?' 'Aye, she's gaun tae the skin works. Better her than me, a couldnae stand that stink. A hae tae haud ma nose just passin' the place, but she says it's better money. They couldnae pay me enough tae get me tae work there'.

Maisie, shuddering at the thought of being a weaver, says 'A couldnae be a weaver either. Aw that terrible noise and shuttles fleein' back and forwards, oh no'.

Martha, looking very agitated, 'Speaking of shuttles, here's one that didn't get across, it jammed in the middle. I've got a smash' (every darners nightmare, it means a big repair job). They all sympathise with her.

Maisie, still thinking of the horrors of the weaving shed, remembers, 'Ma big sister, Betty, tried the weaving a while back. She only lasted the mornin'. She came hame at the denner time. Ma mum asked her how she'd liked it and she started to roar and greet. She was fair breakin' her hert. 'A cannae gaun back, it's awfae, aw' that noise an' they shuttles wizzin. A just cannae go back'. 'Well, ye dinnae hae tae gaun back' says ma mum, 'there's plenty other jobs' ma mum says. 'And that efternin she got a job in Todd the bakers'.

They are all working away when suddenly Jean realises 'Jessie ye never telt us aboot your weekend'. 'Well it wasnae very unusual, I did ma cleanin on Friday night as usual an on Saturday ma Margaret came roond wie the bairns'.

'They must be comin on now' says Lil, 'they are that, Peter's seven, Margo's three and the wee yin is thirteen months. A aye get them their Gala Day outfits, so oo went tae the store. Oo had tae gaun doon in the lift twice or thrice. It's as guid as a shot on the shows tae them, we got them aw kitted oot. A aye keep ma dividend money for this. Then oo had a coffee in Macari's, after that Margaret took the bairns hame while a did ma shoppin. A couldnae believe the queue outside Findlay the butchers. It was doon past the Maypole Dairy doon tae Henry the grocers, aw orderin steak pies for the Gala Day. Mind, they're the best steak pies in the toon'. 'Their mince is awfie guid tae', chips in Cora.

Mock Common Ridings within the mill. Hawick, late 1940's.

Memories of earlier days in Gardiners Mill, Selkirk. circa 1930's.

'Well after shoppin a went hame, a wis never oot at night cos Jock was on duty. Then on Sunday night aw the faimily was in, girlfriends, boyfriends an aw and we aw played ha'penny nap. Oo had a grand laugh, then they aw played cricket doon the lobby while a made the supper. It's a guid job ave got a long lobby'.

Jean looks horrified 'they widnae get tae play cricket in ma hoose, ave got ower mony ornaments tae break'.

Lil has to reply 'aye, an there widnae be sae much fun in a hoose if everybody was watchin the television set'.

Mr Mack comes in carrying a big bale of cloth to be darned 'If yer needles went as fast as yer tongues, oo'd get twice as much work done in here'. The girls are mouthing this behind him, as he says the same thing most days.

Lil, who is not frightened of him and always gives as good as she gets, says 'Oo dinnae darn wie oor mooths Mack, so stop moanin'. 'It's a pity Lil cos yours is big enough'. 'Speakin o big mooths, how's Mrs Mack keepin these days'. 'That's enough back chat frae you Lil.

As a matter o fact she wisnae in guid fettle at aw this weekend, stipid, stipid wuman, ee ken whit she did on Friday night, she was black leedin'

Tea break frolics
at Comelybank
Mill, Galashiels.

Taking a break at
Wilderbank Mill,
Galashiels, 1961.

the grate'. . . Jean, lookin down on anything so old fashioned as a grate. 'Ee didnae still hae a grate sharely. 'O aye she takes great pride in her grate, it's black an shinin like the Earl o Hells waistcoat'.

'Well onyway, she gets it all polished and then throws the empty tin of black leed on the fire wie the lid on, well, ten minutes later there was an almighty explosion and there was black leed everywhere, what a mess, on the wa's, on the ceilin, on the wife, when a came in she was sittin greeting lookin for a the world like Al Jolson. So it was doon tae Mill the painters on Saturday mornin, an a spent the rest o the weekend decoratin, so am no in very guid fettle either, so be warned'. They are all having great difficulty not laughing out loud.

Lil, suppressing her laughter ' well Mack I'll make yer day, there's a thread oot the length o this piece so ye can gie somebody a row, yer favourite job'. Mack, looking at the work tag on the piece of cloth 'Lets see whaes it is, oh her again. Well, am haein her doon here on the carpet this time, she misses far too much'.

As Mack leaves the flat, Lil shakes her head 'power mad, that's what he is, well am away for a fag'.

Maisie jumps up always ready for a skive 'I'll come wie ye Lil'. Jessie decides 'Aye ye can a hae a wee break'. As Cora, Martha and Jean have a chat Rena goes to Jessies table 'can a have a quiet word wi' ee Jessie'. 'Of course ye can lass', movin to the front of the stage where she had her talk with Martha, 'come into my office'.

'Now, what is it hen'. 'A dinnae ken how to tell you this Jessie', 'Jist imagine am yer mum hen'.

'Well it's ma faither, he's started hittin me. It's just when he's drunk Jessie but I dinnae ken how long a can take it'.

'Is he gettin' drunk that often? He never used tae be a heavy drinker'.

'It's just since ma maither died Jessie. A ken he misses her, an awe that, but it wisnae ma fault she died, a miss her tae. Ye ken what he did on Saturday night? Mind a said a got a set hame? Well oo were standin' in the close haein a wee kiss an cuddle, when he comes reelin' along and slaps me across the face, sayin' 'get intae the hoose, ye wee tramp ye, oh Jessie, a was black affronted. A dinnae really ken if that fella will be there on Wednesday night, efter what happened. Well, a got worse when a got in. A dinnae ken how ave no got a keeker the day'.

Jessie gives her hand a pat. 'What a shame hen. Dae yer brothers no dae onything aboot it?'

'Well, they're no usually in. He's aye in first. A think they've got an idea but ye ken what ma faithers like. He rules the roost'.

'A think ma Jock has a pint wie him in the Bridge Inn frae time tae time. A'll hae him hae a word wie yer faither'. Rena looks concerned at this. 'Dinnae worry – he'll dae it in a roondaboot way, him being a polisman, he kens how tae dae such things. Now dinnae worry lass, it'll no' be that long till ye get away frae it aw and stert a new life'.

RENA'S SONG (OVER THERE)

Over there I'm going to find my dream over there
I'll say goodbye to my worries and my cares over there
for I'm young and I'm willing and I'll work all
day long to make my dream come true where
the sky's always blue I'll start my life a new over there
Over there better than my life over here
all the fears all the worry and the tears
over here I want to be free not a
number but me cross the bright shining sea
that's where I want to be
I'll find love just you see over there

Jessie: *Aren't you scared it's so far away*
what'll you do if you don't want to stay
are you sure it's the right way
is it the best thing for you
I only know that sunshine isn't rare over there
I might dare to wear flowers in my hair over there
where men are sublime and their manners are fine
they talk straight from the heart
they're good looking and smart I'll be struck
by cupids dart over there
I'm living by a stream over there and I scream
when I wake up and I'm still over here
is it all make believe how can I really leave
yes I'll make it come true I'll start my life
a new and it's going to be true over there

At the end of her song Rena takes Jessie's hands. 'Aw thanks Jessie. You get awbody's problems. A sometimes wonder whae ye take yours tae'.

Lil and Maisie enter screaming with laughter. Maisie tells them 'what a laugh oo had doon in the lav the now. You tell them Lil'. 'Well, ye ken that daft wee lassie, ye ken, she's no the fu' shillin'. What's her name again Maisie?' Maisie still laughing 'Pamela!'. 'Aye, that's it, Pamela!

Well ye ken they pit up a machine the other day in the lav for the convenience o the weemen. Well she bounces up tae it sayin' 'O guid, a chocolate machine'. 'Then she looks like she's readin it and then says 'Aw no, it's for soap. Everybody in the lav was in stitches'.

Cora, looking very puzzled 'Oh a thought it was a soap machine anaw. Is it no?' This sends them all into fresh peals of laughter.

They all settle back to work. Lil is pulling the cloth over a pole marking the knots with yellow wool ready for the darners to mend. Suddenly, they all jump with surprise as Martha shouts 'I can't stand this any longer, there's hundreds of knots to mend. I could have done without this today. It's just too too much'. She's on the verge of tears.

She stamps over to Rena's table. 'Rena would you give me a cigarette please?' 'But ye dinnae smoke Martha!' She's angry as she says 'Well I feel like one today'. 'Here ye are Martha, will a come wie ye?' 'No thanks, I just want to sit out in the sun for ten minutes by myself' and she slams out. Everyone is amazed, Martha is always so quiet.

Lil is first to speak 'Well she's in some paddy the day is she no'. Jessie is looking very concerned 'Aye, she's got a lot on her mind. She's a worrier is Martha'. Jean says 'her mother and faither are awfae straight laced are they no, Jessie'. 'Aye they are that, very straight laced. A dinnae think there'll be a lot o laughter in that hoose'.

Maisie, who loves to hear the older women tell stories about their younger days, takes this opportunity to get onto one of her favourite subjects 'A dinnae think oo've as much tae worry aboot nowadays as you yins did in the aulden days'. Lil, shocked but with a laugh 'The aulden days, my god, ye make us soond decrepit'. 'A didnae mean it like that, Lil. A just mean aboot the war an afore it. A like when ye tell us aboot they days'. Rena, who also enjoys this topic, encourages them 'So dae a, come on, tell us some'.

The older women are not adverse to this subject and talking helps pass the time more quickly as they darn. Jessie is first to take up the invitation to speak about the 'Aulden Days' "Oh it wasnae aw gloom durin the war. A mean it was bad enough but we had oor lighter moments.

There was yin day a got a parcel frae ma cousin in Canada. Oh it was great tae get a parcel. There was comics and bubble gum for the bairns. Some clathes, which were gie welcome cos o the rationin, and this jar o poodered onion flavouring. Well oo hadnae had ingins for ages. It was a warm summers day so the windaes were open. A pit some o the powder in ma mince and, right enough, the smell jist wafted up – ingins – it wafted right doon the street. In nae time ataw twae o ma neebors came to ma door askin 'Have you got onions Jessie? Where did ee get them?' Well, in the end everybody in the street got a shake o that pooder in there mince or stew that day'.

Rena's early memories are stirred by this story 'It must hae been awfae haein awe they shortages. I can mind o gettin ma first banana. Ma auntie brought it doon frae Edinburgh. A mind runnin roond the street wie it – some o ma pals followin me cos oo had never seen a banana afore, an folk were sayin 'look at that wee lassie, she's got a banana' and they were askin me 'where did ye get it hen'. Then a took it hame. It was gie squashed by then. They were awe sittin in the kitchen and a said 'a dinnae ken how tae

A dern guid holiday, 1956.

open it' an they aw laughed at the thought o a bairn o eight no kennin how tae open a banana'.

Lil quickly takes up the story, telling 'A can mind, can you Jean?, o paintin a black line doon the back o oor legs tae make it look like oo had stockins on. Oo yist tae stan on a chair while yer pal painted the line. Then the Canadians came – they aye had nylons. Ye wid hae done onythin (she looks at Jean) well almost onythin for a pair o nylons'.

Jean gives a Hmmm and then picks up the tale 'Oh! thae Canadians'. Then, explaining to the young ones 'It was Canadians, no Yanks, that came tae Gala for their leave. They got billeted in the Douglas Hotel. Div ye ken what they did yin night? They uplifted aw the hotel carpets and selt them. They got up tae some pranks, thae lads'.

Maisie, wanting to tell her young memories of the war, joined in 'A can just mind, cos a was only five or six, gaun up tae the Peel Hospital wie the Winnie Haig Dancers tae dae a concert. A think Davie Ferguson got it the gether for the wounded sodgers. Ave got lots o their autographs in ma book, they were frae aw our the world. Canada, Poland and yin Irish man wrote 'I can't say I'm Irish now as they pumped a lot of Scot's blood into me at Peel'.

'Oh aye, ye couldnae beat the Poles', says Lil with a knowing smile. 'They had such lovely manners. They stood up when ye came into a room an clicked their heels (she demonstrates). When ye were introduced, some o them kissed yer hand. They made ye feel a real lady'.

Jean gives a snort. 'Is that what your Peter was like Lil' asks Rena. 'Oh aye, he was. He just swept me off ma feet'. 'But Peter's a British name Lil!' 'His real name is Pietrich'. Maisie, all dreamy asks 'Was it love at first sight, Lil?' 'It was that. Oor eyes met across the dance flair, the Palais, of course. He came across, clicked his heels, kissed ma hand an a was a goner'.

'Was it long afore ye got mairried?' 'Aboot three months. Oo had to get special permission but, come hell or high water, Peter was determined tae mairry me. Div ye ken, for the first year Peter never saw me without ma make-up on. A used tae get up half an oor afore him every day, jist tae get glammed up'. Jean, under her breath 'Silly bitch'.

Cora, with an inspired look recites 'A little dab o pooder, a little dab o paint, makes a greasy derner, look like what she ain't'. Lil looks at Cora and her mouth falls open. For once she hasn't got an answer.

Jean thinks this is hilarious and leans towards Cora 'My that was a guid yin Cora, a right guid yin'. Rena, wanting to know the rest of the romantic story asks 'You still seem to be jist as happy now Lil'. 'Yes, a am that. He's a guid man. Mind, a little Pietrich would hae been awfae nice but oo were never blessed'.

Jessie, looking at the clock 'Martha's been an awfae long time'. Lil replies 'Well a hope Mack hasnae noticed she's been oot as long, cos it'll no matter tae him if she's yin o the quiet yins. He'll come doon on her like a ton o bricks'. 'Aye', Cora says, 'a leopard disnae change his stripes, he's the same wi them aw'.

Jean wonders 'Does she never gaun oot wi you young yins, and hae a guid time?' 'She's been oot a couple o times wie us, hasn't she Maisie?' 'Aye, but she took a lot o persuadin. A think if she took a drink she might relax a wee bit. Oo'll see if oo can get her oot this woolkend an cheer her up'. Jessie thinks this is a guid idea 'That wid be nice girls, see what ye can dae'.

Lil glances at the clock 'Thank God it's nearly denner time'. They all start to take off their tweed aprons (scoojies) and gather up their bags as Jessie tells them 'Ma nceber's pittin ma tatties on for me, so they'll be jist aboot ready when a get in'. 'That saves a lot o time, dae they awe come hame for their denner Jessie?' asks Jean.

'Some days, but Jock's on duty the day an Bill's workin oot o the toon'.

As she is saying this Mr Mack bursts through the door to the centre of the flat. He is dripping wet 'Jessie, ee had better come wie me. Ave just tane Martha oot o the dam'. They are all horrified and everybody runs out the door.

END OF ACT ONE

Act Two

Wednesday, after lunch, a few minutes before the hooter, Maisie and Rena are looking at and admiring Maisie's Gala Day outfit. Cora arrives carrying a large brown box and seeing the nice things says 'Oh! that looks nice Maisie'. Lil is right behind her 'Oh good Maisie, ye've brought yer outfit, ye'll hae tae let us see it on'.

Jean and Jessie enter together. Jessie goes to look at Maisie's skirt. 'My, my, that looks lovely Maisie'. Jean is putting her apron on 'The young yins are that lucky nowadays. There's some lovely clathes in the shops'.

As Jessie puts on her apron she goes over to Cora 'Hallo Cora!, did ye hae a guid denner?'

'Oh!, aye it was awfae guid. Some days a cannae be bothered cookin for ma'sel, an the day was yin o them, so a went tae Chamberlains Cafe. A had three courses an it was only two and sixpence. It was beautiful. By the time a buy aw the stuff, an cook it, a cannae dae it much cheaper'.

'Aw, yer quite right Cora'.

Jessie claps her hands to get everyone's attention 'Listen everybody, Martha's comin in this efternin. A met her mother when a was doon the street. She says she's a lot better, an nane the worse for fawin in the dam'. They are all relieved to hear this news. 'That's guid' says Rena 'ool hae tae try and cheer her up'.

Lil, calling a spade a spade as usual 'A hope oo can aw cheer up, it's been like a bloody morgue in here since Monday'. Maisie thinks this a great idea 'Aye, let's get the Gala Week feeling back again.

Go an try yer outfit on Maisie, there's a few meenits tae the hooter'. 'Div ye think a should Lil'. Everyone encourages her and she goes off to put it on.

As they wait for her, Jessie tells them what she did in the dinner break 'A managed tae nip roond and see Nellie Henderson for a minnit'. 'Was she aw right' enquires Jean. 'She had an awfae bad bang on the heid, another inch an she wid hae lost an eye'. Lil asks 'Did she see a doctor?'. 'Aye, Dr Weatherhead was in tae see her'. 'What did he say?'. They all look at each other and say as one 'TAKE TWAE ASPRINS' and then laugh.

Just then Martha comes in looking a bit embarrassed 'Hallo everybody'. Jessie goes over to her and puts an arm round her 'Hallo Martha, it's grand tae see ye back'. Jean enquires 'Are ye OK hen?'. Martha, looking sheepish 'I feel such a fool'.

Jean, wanting all the details 'What happened onyway, Martha?'. Everyone was listening.

'Well I went to sit beside the dam to smoke the cigarette. Everybody seems to light up when they have a crisis, so I thought it might help. I wasn't enjoying it one bit, and I felt a bit sick, but I kept going till the end. Then, when I stood up my head was spinning and I was so dizzy. Then the next thing I remember was Mr Mack bringing me round' 'For ye e' says Lil 'Oo should he glad auld "Hawkeen" noticed ye were away longer than

E.Y. Johnstone's Burns' Supper, with the late Henry Polson, Gala's first Braw Lad of (1930) – 1952.

ye should hae been'. Jessie agrees 'Aye! it's a blessin that he went lookin for ye'. 'He saved my life Jessie'. 'He did that, Hen'.

As she is saying this she is leading Martha to the corner of the flat (her office) out of ear shot 'An how are ye besides that'. 'I'm fine Jessie. After all my fuss it was a false alarm. I'm OK, thank goodness'. 'Am that glad Martha, ye'll hae tae try an no worry sae much aboot things. Ee want to get oot wi the lasses this weekend and enjoy yersel'. 'I think I will Jessie'.

Maisie arrives singing and dancing and twirling round to best show off her wide skirt and frilly petticoat. She grabs Martha's hands and they dance together.

The hooter sounds and Mr Mack walks in 'What the bloody hell's gaun on in here. This isnae the bloody Palais de Dance ye ken. Yer supposed tae be startin tae work when the hooter gauns'.

Lil, who is always ready to tackle him 'Gie's a break Mack, it's the Gala Week. Ye ken spirits run high and hearts flutter this week'.

'Thae young yins nowadays dinnae ken what hard work is, they get a'thing that easy. It wasnae like that when a was a laddie'.

Maisie, being quite brave 'A cannae imagin you young, Mr Mack'. 'Oh! but he was' says Jessie. 'A can mind when he left the schill'. Cora smiles at Mack, saying 'And a fine handsome upright young laddie he was tae'. Mr Mack is not adverse to a bit of flattery and they all know this. He puffs his chest out and looks pleased.

Jeans joins in the play 'He was that Cora.

Ye started work as an apprentice undertaker wie the Co-op, a mind'.

Cora, giggling 'That must have been bury nice'.

'Was that no a kind o depressin job Mr Mack?' asks Rena. 'Every job has it's lighter moments, Rena'.

Mr Mack is still enjoying the attention he is receiving until Cora starts to remember something from his past 'Was it no you that was in the paper'. Lil starts to laugh 'Oh! aye, the coffin, oh! that was a laugh'.

Maisie desperately wants to know 'Oh tell us, tell us'. Mr Mack gives Lil a thunderous look 'LIL!!'. Lil winks to the girls 'At the break then'. Again Mr Mack shouts 'LIL!!'. Jessie jumps to his rescue 'Stop teasin girls, you'd best tell it yersel Mr Mack'. 'Aye' says Cora 'Lil wid maybe excruciate it'. Jean quickly corrects her 'Exaggerate'. 'And you ken awe aboot that' retorts Lil. 'Come on Mr Mack, tell the girls yer story'.

'Aw right then. It wasnae that funny though. Yin day a was bringin this coffin frae a hoose in Stirling Street tae the undertakers – nae cars in they days, it was a horse and cairt – an a was gaun up Bank Street brae. A was jist aboot at the top when a laddie on a bike came whizzin doon Gala Park Road an gliffed the horse. It reared up an the coffin shot doon the hill like a roller coaster, right across the road and intae Davie Ferguson's the draper. It hit the coonter wie a thud an the lid flew off. Withoot a blink, Davie Ferguson, leaned ower the coonter and says "Wis ye no pleased wie that last suit a made ye Mr Thomson".

They all erupt in laughter. Rena is first to recover 'Yer haein us on Mr Mack'. Lil, holding her sides 'Naw, it's true, hc disnae hae enough sense o humour tae make up a funny story'.

'Nane o yer lip Lil, just aw get back tae work' and he stomps out. Lil, looking in the direction he has left 'A forgot. He disnae hae a heart, jist a swingin chuckle stane. He disnae ken how tae hae fun'. Cora has another gem of wisdom 'All work and no fun makes Jock a dull boy'. 'Play and Jack, Cora!'.

Martha, who has cheered up considerably 'Well I'm getting into the Gala Day feeling. I'm beginning to understand it a bit better now. I tell Ian

Ordeal for the bride to be. Lochcarron Mill, Galashiels.

41

all about it in my letters'. 'Does he come frae Huddersfield anaw, Martha' asks Cora. 'Yes he does'. Jean, curious as ever 'Will ye gaun an live there when ye get mairried?' 'Yes, Ian's got quite a good job in one of the big mills there, but I'll be getting married here'. Jessie is very pleased 'O good, oo'll be able tae come and see ye on yer weddin day'.

There's a lull in the conversation as they continue to work but Jean is ready for some gossip 'Here Lil, oo came up the road wi Janet Wilson the now. What a face she's got, hasn't she, Jessie?' 'She hasnae half, puir lassie, she's got twae black een'. Lil is incensed 'Has that pig o a man been hittin her again. Ye ken, if he was mine a'd swing for him'.

Enjoying a good gossip, Jean continues 'What a life she's had wie him. Div ee mind last year at the Gala Day, he got that drunk doon at the sports, he was pickin a fight we onybody that was near him. In the end, the Polis took him in an he spent the night under the clock' (police station).

'A ken yin o his lassies' Maisie tells them 'an she hasnae much o a life neether. The last time a was talkin tae her, she was thinkin o daein the same as you, Rena'.

A ken how she feels. A'll hae tae gie her some o the addresses a wrote tae'.

Looking pained, Jean states 'Mind, some weemen dinnae half suffer at the hands o men'. They all consider this statement and nod heads in agreement.

Then Lil remembers a story she once heard 'A hae a cousin up in Glesgae, an she telt me this story yince. She had a really guid pal that was being battered regularly by this pig tae beat aw pigs. Every week there was somethin. He pit her in hospital twice. She had four wee bairns and she got hardly ony money frae him. There was this yin day, it was that cauld the bairns were freezin, an he wuidnae gie her money for coal. So when he went tae the pub, an they were left in the cauld hoose, in sheer desperation she sawed the legs off the table and pit them on the fire so she could warm the bairns. When he came hame that was another batterin! – Another time – it was the fifth o November, ma cousin and this pal took the bairns tae a bonfire and fireworks. Well, on the way back she says tae ma cousin "Come on up for a cup o tea". They lived in yin o thae tenements. "He's in" she says "but it's ok, he's aye nice when there's onybody else aroond". So up they go – an she keeps the key hingin inside the letter box – she lifts the flap tae get the key an the smell o gas that came oot was overpowerin!'.

They have all stopped work and are listening with baited breath.

'She puts doon the letter box very very carefully, looks at ma cousin, an says quietly "Can oo gaun tae yer hoose for a cuppa tea?" an they did'.

All gasp and say 'Oh! no, never'. Maisie urges her 'What happened next, Lil?' then Rena 'Come on Lil, tell us what happened'. Lil continues the story.

'Well, they had their tea and went back tae the hoose, twae oors later'. She looks at them to see their reaction. 'An he was deid'. Again they react with 'Good Grief. A cannae believe it. That's terrible'.

Lil goes on 'When ma cousin telt me this story she said "A don't know if a did the right thing that day, Lilian, it's aye been on ma conscience". An a said "Is the lassie ony happier" and she said "Oh aye, she mairried a guid man twae years later an she's never looked back" so a says "There's yer answer then, a widnae lose a meenits sleep ower it. That pig got what he deserved".

'For yince a cnn igree wie ye Lil' says Jean. They are all very thoughtful about Lil's tale. 'Oo'r awfae lucky' says Cora 'Livin in a nice wee toon. Some o they folk in the big cities hae an awfae life o it'. Maisie, nearly in tears 'Fancy havin tae saw the legs off the table tae keep the wee bairns warm. Puir wee things'.

'Mind Cora, it's no just the big cities that have got bast. . .' she stops and quickly corrects herself 'bad men in them, Janet Wilson will testify tae that'.

Martha has had enough of doom and gloom 'Let's talk about something nice now. I was in such a good mood when I came in'.

'Aye' jokes Lil 'Oo did kindae notice the difference frae Monday! Did ee win the pools or even better get a letter frae Ian?' 'Yes, somethin like that, Lil' she smiles at Jessie.

They go on working as they think of the next topic and Martha is first to come up with one 'Anyone know what show the opera society are doing this year?'

This subject is close to Maisie's heart 'No but, Oh, a wid love tae join the Opera but a dinnae ken how tae go aboot it'.

Cora can help here. 'Ma niece Muriel's in it Maisie, she could probably get ye in'.

'That would be brilliant, Cora, a've been gaun tae see it since a was wee. It was 'The Belle of New York' this year. It was just great. That John Leishman and Jessie Grieve are smashin singers'. Dreamily she says 'A wid jist love tae gaun on the stage.

MAISIE'S SONG "STAGESTRUCK"

They say I have talent what do they mean
could I be a star of the silver screen
could I dance or sing on the stage
could I be all the rage
could I be like Doris Day
could I sing on moonlight bay
could I be like Judy so I'd sing
ore the rainbow
could I dance in a chorus line
or with Gene Kelly that would be fine
no I couldn't do that it wouldn't be fair
not on poor Fred Astaire
I'm just a darner but in here
I've got such a longing for a stage career
could it happen have I got what it takes
I think I could if I got the breaks

Jean continues 'A like the opera tae. They put on a grand show divent they, Cora?'

'Well ye ken what they say Jean, there's no business like funny business'. Lil laughs 'You can say that again Cora'. Cora is just about to say it again as instructed 'There's no business. . ..' when Jean stops her 'Only kiddin Cora'.

Jessie changes the subject 'A thought ye were bringin in yer weddin dress tae let us see, Cora?' 'An so a have, it's here'. They are all enthusiastic to see it, especially Martha 'I'm dying to see it Cora, I love old wedding dresses'.

'You might'n be able tae dae onythin wie it Martha, but a kindae like the idea o it gettin yased efter aw they years lyin in a box. Mind a take it oot yince a year on the third o September and hae a wee look at it and refold it in a different way' she is untying the string on the box as she talks 'so that it disnae get marked. 'Ye couldnae hae a dress that's had mair love put intae it than this yin'. She unfolds the dress from the box and there are gasps of delight from all, it's a beautiful dress.

Martha is almost in tears 'Oh! Cora, it's the loveliest wedding dress I've ever seen, I can't believe it'.

'Angus bought it for me in Paris. It was frae yin o the top fashion hooses'.

Martha is still stunned 'It looks so new and so perfect'.

'Well ave looked efter it'. 'It's like oot a film' gasps Maisie 'When did ee get it Cora?' 'It was 1917, on his last leave hame'.

They all go back to work as they listen to Cora. She sits down cradling her dress 'The first night a met Angus, oo'd been at a church Kinderspiel and there was a dance efter it. He comes ower tae me an says 'can I have the pleasure of this dance, Miss Lynch?'. Ye could hae knocked me doon wie a feather – he was frae a different class o folk a' thegether – a was fair dumbfounded. 'How div ye ken ma name?' says I. 'I've known your name for a long time', says he. 'I used to see you in church every Sunday and I couldn't keep my eyes off you, but then I had to go to University, so I haven't seen you for a long time'.

He was that handsome, he had the darkest broon een a've ever seen, they were almost black and he had the warmest smile, wie fine even white teeth. Well he danced me for the rest o the night and it didnae seem tae mitter that a didnae talk posh. Mind a maybe didnae talk as broad as a normally do, ye dinnae when yer talkin tae somebody posh, div ye? They widnae understand ye, wid they?

Well at the end o the dance he asked me if he could walk me hame. Ma heid was in a spin, a cannae let him ken, a live up a close, up a stair in an attic – can a? Yer heids that fu o foolish pride when yer young, so onyway a says 'a live in Scott Crescent' so oo walks up that way an a' stops at the big hoose next tae the Scott Park gates.

Well oo stood and blethered aboot this an that and made arrangements tae meet again, then he opens the gate tae let me in. A was fair worried that somebody wid come oot the hoose. 'Well goodnight Angus', I says, 'Goodnight Cora, thank you for a lovely evening, and by the way, when you go into that house, will you give my regards to my Aunt Catherine'. I wanted the ground tae swallow me up – it was ma maist embarrasin' moment. Then he started tae laugh, and oo laughed a the way up tae the top o Scott Street.'

They all laugh, Maisie thinks of Cora's embarrassment 'What a red face tae get'. Lil, still laughing 'Oh! that was a guid yin Cora'. 'It was right romantic in a way though' muses Rena 'it showed he wasnae a snob'. Martha, still with tears in her eyes 'That was a lovely story, Cora'.

Jean has stopped work and leans towards Cora. She is very interested to hear about a posh family 'So whae is his faimily and what job did he have'.

'Oh he didnae hae a job Jean, he had a profession, he was a lawyer'. Jean's eyebrows shoot up, she is very impressed. 'His faither had a lawyer's business in the toon, McFarlin and Freeman. Angus McFarlin he was.

We had a wonderful summer that year. It was 1913. Oo went picnics and long long walks, ma favourit was up Gala Hill. Then the day came that a had been dreadin!'

Maisie, in a very serious voice, says 'He had tae go tae the war?'

'Naw, naw, a had to meet his faimily. Angus was determined tae get engaged, so a was tae gaun this Sunday for ma tea.

Oo went for a walk first, then oo got tae his hoose. It was up Parsonage Road. His mother took ma hat and coat and a said 'How do you do' tae his faither and there were twae aunts and uncles' there. His mother says 'I hope that long walk has given you young people an appetite' and a says 'oh yes, am absolutely ravishing'. Well they a started tae laugh – Angus an naw. He said to them 'I told you how wonderful she is. Is she not the sweetest thing you've ever seen'. Well whatever they were laughin at, it broke the ice. They were that nice to me, no snobbish at a'.

Jean, wanting even more details 'Did they hae a really posh hoose Cora?'

'Did they no jist, Jean. Sitting room, dining room, we real paintins on the wall. And' she emphasises to Jean ' twae bathrooms'. Jean rolls her eyes at such luxury. 'A have never seen a hoose like it. The table was beautifully set wie lovely china, a silver tea set and yin o they big silver condom sets'. Everybody gasps, the young ones giggle. Jean, knowing the proper name for such things corrects her 'A condiment set Cora!' 'Aye, yin o thae.

So then his mother says "We're having Bombay Duck, Cora. I hope you like that". "Oh yes!" says I "I love it". A've had chicken and a thought, well, duck cannae be that different. Well, when she brings in the dish and takes the lid off, she must have seen ma face faw cos it wisnae duck, it was fish'. "Do you not like fish, Cora?" she says. "A thought you said it was duck, but a must have been wrong". Well they aw laughed again and then he gave me a wee hug'.

'So it seems like they fair took tae ye, Cora' says Jessie. 'Oh aye, a got on fine wie them. A seemed tae make them laugh, sometimes a wisnae share why'.

Lil, not sure if they had been laughing with her, or at her 'Ye never felt Cora, that they were lookin doon on ye?'

'Oh no!, no, Angus wuidnae hae taken me there if they had. No, they were just nice folk, in fact, it was his mother suggested he get ma dress in France'.

Martha, really enjoying this romantic tale 'They sound like nice people, Cora, what happened next?'

Cora pauses and gives a sigh 'The war – that's what happened next. He came hame on his last leave from France with this beautiful dress. He was an officer ye ken. He took me on four days holiday to Helensburgh. A never saw him again efter that leave – but a've go some lovely memories'.

CORA'S SONG – LOVELY MEMORIES

I've got lovely memories o such lovely memories
of a time so long ago of a lassie and her beau
we were lithe young and gay so alike in every way
but our lives were worlds apart
I've got lovely memories o such lovely memories
no I wasn't always old I was young and I was bold
my boy dear to me to hold close and near to me
o so long ago
Oh those Sunday mornings sunlit Sunday mornings
walks upon the hills it seemed to me that time stood still
dancing till the dawn kisses sweet and long
like our life would be
I've got lovely memories o such lovely memories
of a love so deep and true that it filled me
through and through and so inside I died with you
o so long ago

Everyone is very close to tears. Cora gets up from her seat, lays her dress down, very carefully and gently, and heads for the door to the toilets. As she reaches the door she slowly turns round and says 'A ken what they say aboot auld spinster Cora – will she die wonderin – well it's nae secret ony mair – a wunnae'.

This immediately brings a smile to everyone's lips as they dab their eyes, then Jessie issues the order 'What Cora said the now doesn't get repeated outside these walls'. All nod in agreement.

Mack arrives with a weaver behind him. She looks very embarrassed and a bit frightened. He takes her to the cloth hanging over the poles where Lil works. 'This is the second time a've had ye doon here Sadie. There's a threed oot nearly the hale length o this wobe an mair shots than a can coont. What have ye got tae say for yersel?'

Sadie, in a tremulous voice 'It's an awfie fine piece Mr Mack. A think maybe am needin tae get some glesses'. 'Glesses lassie, it's a bloody white stick yere needin! A blind man runnin for a bus could o seen that. If a hae tae hae ye doon here again, Sadie, ye'll be gettin yer cairds. Now get back tae the weavin shed an pay mair attention tae yer work'.

Sadie leaves with her head down. Mr Mack goes over to Lil 'Now mind a want tae ken if she has anither bad wobe, Lil'.

As he is walking out of the door, Lil is shouting after him 'Oh aye, make me the bloody high executioner. A hope he disnae think am gaun tae be the cause o that puir lassie loosin her job.

They are all quietly working and Maisie, who can't stand long spells of silence, just has to talk 'Are ye no gettin right excited aboot gaun tae America, Rena?'

'A am Maisie' 'They say awbodys' got phones in their hooses' 'The folk am gaun tae hae a swimmin pool' There are oo's and ah's all round 'an a've tae get the use o a car on ma day off'.

Jean snaps 'But ye dinnae drive, Rena!' 'A ken Jean, but a can learn' 'Huh, fancy that'

'What will yer job entail, hen?' asks Jessie,

'Lookin efter their twae wee lassies, and another baby due in December, and some light hoosework'.

Lil, more to get Jean going than out of interest 'A suppose they'll hae a refrigerator an a washin machine'. As she knew she would, Jean takes the bait again 'A've got ma washin machine so a think ma next purchase will be a refrigerator'. Lil gives a smile of triumph and says in a rather posh voice 'The prices of these things are coming down all the time. Soon us lesser mortals will be able to afford them'.

Rena decides to join in Lils fun 'By the letters, they seem like an awfae nice faimily, an div ye ken what else?' she looks directly at Jean, 'am tae hae ma ane room wie a bathroom'. Jean rolls her eyes and sighs 'Ma life will be complete when a hae ma bathroom pit in'. They smile knowingly at each other.

'Well a'm looking forward tae ma new life'. Looking at the clock, she goes on 'A wish Molly wid come for me. Am gaspin for a fag'. 'Div ye mean Molly Dickson', asks Jessie 'wie the different coloured een, or Molly Patterson?' 'Molly Dickson', replies Rena.

Jean is alert at once, this is something she hasn't heard of 'Different coloured een! What div ye mean, Rena?'

'She's got yin blue and yin broon'.

Cora is amazed 'Yin blue and yin broon, a've never heard the likes o that afore'.

'Neither have a. A've spoke tae that lassie and a've never noticed afore. When she comes in Rena, say yer no ready an gie Cora an I a chance tae hae a wee look'

Well, dinnae make it obvious that yer lookin mind Jean' 'Of course a winnae'.

Martha, still in a good mood 'I think it looks very attractive – well different anyway'. Jean is thinking 'It must be difficult for her', 'In what way Jean' wonders Rena. 'Well, when yer choosin a frock or a blouse tae match yer eyes'. 'Aw Jean' Rena exclaims.

Maisie, in a dreamy voice 'Elizabeth Taylor's got violet eyes'.

'A dinnae think a ken her, does she work in this mill?' Cora asks.

Maisie doesn't bother to explain but asks Rena 'what night are ye gaun tae the shows Rena?', 'A think it'll be Thursday night, div ye gaun Cora?', 'Oh aye a like tae hae a walk roond, a miss no haein a bairn tae take. Ma niece Muriels' aw growin up now'.

Jessie suggests 'Ye can take twae o ma grand bairns Cora. It costs a fortune tae take them. Thrupence a go, when there's three it's gie dear, mind a fair enjoy it'.

Molly puts her head round the door 'are ye gaun for a fag Rena?', Rena looking guilty, 'can ye wait a meenit Molly, am at an awfae tricky bit'. Jean goes to the door and takes Molly by the arm. 'Come on in, come and see Cora's lovely dress Molly', Cora joins in the persuasion, 'Aye Molly come an hae a wee look hen'. All the time they are talking to Molly they are looking intently into her eyes, much to Renas' disgust. Molly too is very suspicious of their motives, she looks at Coras' dress. 'This is beautiful Cora, a didnae ken you were ever mairried.'

Cora is still trying to get a better look into her eyes, 'Naw, but a nearly was, so a keep it jist in case'. Then suddenly she gets a good look and shouts 'Oh, so ye have!' Molly draws back and is not too pleased 'So a have what?'. Cora looks pleadingly at Jean to get her out of trouble, Jean thinking rapidly comes up with, 'Got awfae nice perfume on, Rena wis jist sayin Molly aye has awfae nice perfume on'. Cora exaggeratingly sniffing 'Oh aye, it's awfae, awfae nice'. Molly giving them both a suspicious look 'Are ye ready Rena, oor wastin smokin time', 'Aye am ready now' and leaves giving them a dirty look and shaking her fist at them. Maisie ready for another skive 'I'll come wie ye'.

Jean thrilled that she had seen Mollys' eyes 'Well did ye see them Cora?', 'A did that, there was definitely yin blue and yin broon', 'a've never seen that afore, did ye ken they were like that Jessie?', 'Aye a've kent her since she was a bairn. A yist tae be quite pally wi her mother'.

Christmas Dinner E. Y. Johnstone's. 1951.

Cora's wedding dress. Rideout Theatre Company, 1994.

'What Dicksons are they then, the yins frae Plumtree?', 'Naw, naw the yins frae Lintburn Street', Jean, wanting still more info 'What was her mother's name afore she was mairried?' Jessie has to think 'Er! Er! Fairbairn – Aye! Fairbairn'. Oh! aye, a've got ye now'. Now Cora wants to know 'Was that the Fairbairns frae the Auld Toon Cross way cos, if it was, a kent her granny'. Lil bangs a cone of wool on the table 'Let's stop his conversation now, afore oor bloody three hundred years back in the history o Gala'.

Martha tries to lighten things 'Would you like a sweetie ladies?' Cora looks surprised 'It's no Friday is it?' No Cora, it's not, I just felt like a celebration' as she starts to hand them round. Cora, needing a good excuse to have a sweet on any other day but Friday 'Because it's Gala week then', 'Yes, that's right Cora'. As she takes a sweetie, Lil says 'You definitely got good news since Monday! Just watch, that Mack will be in in a meenit, he can hear a sweetie paper at twae hundred yerds'.

'Are ye gaun tae try the dress on, Martha?' asks Jessie. 'I would love to', she turns to Cora 'are you sure about this Cora?' 'Aye, a'm very sure. It was bought tae make a lassie happy and it's aboot time it did it's job.' Martha gives Cora a hug 'It will certainly do that'. Jessie tells her 'Away an get intae it, the lassies should be back by then'.

Mr Mack walks in and they all start to laugh and Lil says 'What did a tell ye, a kent it ' they're still laughing.

Mack, angrily 'What are ye awe laughin at'.

'Martha just went roond wie the sweeties an a said ye wid hear the paper rustle.

'It's no Friday, is it?' 'No!' 'Whae's got the sweeties then' he gets one from Martha 'A'll take yin for efter an awe'.

Looking round the flat 'Where are thae young yins, as if a didnae ken'. Jessie quickly defends them 'They've only jist went' 'Dinnae tell me they jist went – a ken fine when they went, an they've got aboot a meenit an a half tae get back. It's aye the same, the week afore Christmas, the week afore the Trades holiday an the week afore the Gala Day. There seems tae be some sort o madness gets intae them. Ma life's no worth livin thae weeks'. He picks up a big roll of tweed that has just been darned, puts it on his shoulder and makes to go out 'They'd better hurry up, a've got Gledstanes the shrinkers tae gaun tae'.

As he is leaving, the girls nearly knock him down, 'Sorry Mr Mack' apologises Rena. 'Dinnae sorry me ma lass. How long div ye caw this tae be oot for a smoke?' Maisie answers back a bit cheekily 'Oo've only been a couple o meenits'. 'A couple o meenits ma fit, nane o yer cheek, just watch yer time in future', on this he leaves. Lil, shaking her head 'He really is power mad, that man. Rena, you go an tell Martha she can come oot now, oo dinnae hae tae worry, Hitler's away tae the shrinkers'.

Rena holds the door open for Martha, who is looking beautiful in the dress 'Well then, what do you think'. They all speak at once 'Oh beautiful hen!' 'Oh Martha!, you're lovely' 'Isn't it smashing' 'It's oot of this world'. Jean as usual, doesn't like giving too much praise 'It's no what's in the fashion at the meenit' everyone gives her a dirty look 'but a've got tae admit – it's really, really nice'.

Cora, dabbing her eyes 'Martha, Martha, am awfie pleased a got it oot for ye. Ye look that nice. A never tried it on, so this is the first time a've seen it properly. Turning to everybody 'It's lovely, isn't it?' They all smile and nod in agreement. 'I can't thank you enough Cora, you've made my dreams come true. I want you to be a very special guest at my wedding – will you?' 'That would be very nice Martha, thank you'.

Jessie, near to tears too 'Ye'd better take it off hen, afore it gets dirty' 'OK Jessie'. They watch her go and Maisie says 'Wasn't she lovely?' Rena gives a little shudder 'It fair made me awe goose pimples'. Cora is very thoughtful and has never taken her eyes off the door that Martha went out. To no-one in particular, she says 'A think a'll help her take it off' and follows her.

'Puir Cora' says Maisie 'fancy never haein it on' 'What a shame' agrees Rena. 'She wid hae looked beautiful in it, tae. She was awfae good lookin as a lassie'. Jessie tells the girls 'mind, Lil, when she brought some photos in a few years ago, ye could see how lovely she'd been'. 'Oh aye!, she was that'.

Maisie, excitedly says 'That wid be a brilliant idea'. Jean looks puzzled 'What wid?'. Bringin in auld photographs. A love lookin at auld photos, especially o the aulden days' she ducks and Lil scuffs her head, playfully. 'Am only kiddin, Lil!' 'Aulden days eh!' 'It's a guid idea though' Jean agrees. 'Oo'll awe bring photaos in the morn – some when oo were bairns an awe Oo'll plt them on the table and guess whae's whae'. Lil, who never misses a chance to remind Jean of her beginnings 'Aye, you and I will be the yins wie oor breek erses hingin oot, eh Jean!'.

Maisie, curious as ever ' Was it awfae bad in the aulden – a mean – when you yins were wee?'

'Well, oo didnae ken it was bad – did oo Jean? Oo had nothin else tae judge it wie, awbody was in the same boat'. 'Naw oo didnae. Oo still had lots o guid fun. The summer's seemed longer then, oo never had shoes on oor feet awe summer'.

'That was cos oor mothers couldnae bloody afford them. They could jist afford shoes for the winter'.

'Div ye mind, Lil? Oo yist tae hae rare picnics up the Rye Haugh'.

'Picnics?, a bottle o water an a jam piece'.

'Aye, yer right enough. There was yin day, a mind, ma mother and faither tane us up Buckholm Hill for a picnic. There was only aboot eight o us bairns at the time. Well oo were sittin aboot half way up, lookin ower Gala, an ma mother said "There's an awfae smell o smoke" and oo turned roond an is the hale hill no ablaze and headin towards us? Oo had tae gether aw oor stuff up an run doon the hill. Ye ken what had happened? Twae o ma brothers had tane ma faither's matches an set the whin alight. What a leatherin they got, a can tell ye'.

'Did I hear Lil say there was thirteen in your family Jean?' 'Aye, there was, an oo awe lived in twae rooms an a kitchen'. 'My god' exclaims Rena.

Wakefield Mill, 1950's.

'Aye, it was a tight squeeze. It wasnae jist twae or three tae a bed, it was fower or five'.

Lil is surprised at Jean telling about her young life and hardships and gives her a chance to boast, as she knows she will 'But it didnae dae them ony herm Jean, did it?' 'No, they're awe in awfie, awfie, guid jobs now. Twae o ma brothers an three o ma sisters are in Canada now, awe daein awfae weel. Twae o them are comin hame next year for the Gala Day. Oo've no seen each other for mair than – o it must be sixteen years'.

'Is it your John that's comin hame Jean?' 'Aye, John and Greta'.

'Here, div ye mind Jean, when she was oor apprentice derner here and ower the Gala week oo did the ceremony o the mixin o the roses here in the flat, an she took the pairt o the Braw Lass'.

Cora, who has just come in and caught the end of the conversation, tells them 'Aye, and a mind Mr Mack was the Braw Lad'. The girls look at her in disbelief, and Lil tells them 'Aye, that was afore he lost his sense o humour' and Jessie adds 'Of course he wasnae a gaffer then'.

Rena says 'That soonds really guid fun'. Maisie, full of enthusiasm 'Oh let's dae it again, please, a want somethin tae be able tae look back on an tell ma bairns aboot'. Jessie, warming to the idea 'Oo have nae din it for years' looking at Lil ' div ye think oo should?' 'Oh aye! – what the hell. It'll be guid fun'. Jean, amazingly agreeing with Lil ' A think oo should anaw. Oo should keep the traditions gaun for the young yins'.

Mr Mack comes in, carrying another bale of cloth for darning. Lil makes right over to him and in a cajoling voice 'Oo were jist reminiscin aboot the time oo did the 'Mixin of the Roses' ceremony a few years ago, div ye mind?' Giving it a lot of thought 'Oh aye!, a mind', then with a broad smile and sticking his chest out 'A was the Braw Lad' 'Well wid ye like tae be him again?' The smile disappears 'yer bloody joking – aren't ye Lil?', 'No', 'Dinnae be sae daft Lil' 'Awe, come on Mack – for the young yins. Show them ye've no aye been a dour, soor faced, auld bugger'.

Before he can give Lil a row for her cheek, Maisie and Rena are pleading with him 'please Mr Mack' 'Go on Mr Mack, oo'll work right hard the morn'. Cora joins in 'Martha's never seen the ceremony. We were tryin tae describe it, but it wid be better if oo could show her'. Jean tries strong flattery 'And oo need somebody wie authority tae be the Braw Lad'. Jessie adds for good measure 'Ye'll get double sweeties on Friday'. This clinches it. 'Aw right ye daft buggers, a'll be back in five meenits, you get it organised.' They are all thrilled and shout their thanks to him as he leaves.

Lil takes charge, giving orders for what they need. 'Right, oo'll need a pole for the Braw Lads flag, this'll dae. Now gies yer scoogie Jean, you tie that on tae the pole for a flag. Cora, you get us cushions for the sod and the stane an somethin tae represent the roses. Martha and Rena, you help me clear a space for the platform, and you Maisie, you go an get Molly and er.. Sadie, cos oo need ten for the ceremony.' There's much activity as they all get ready and when they are all assembled Lil puts them all in the right places for the start of the ceremony with Cora as the Braw Lass and Mr Mack the Braw Lad.

They perform the ceremony with serene dignity as it is performed on the Gala Day. Jessie sings 'Sweet Lass of Richmond Hill'. When the ceremony is over, they call for three cheers for the Laird o' Gala.

They are all laughing and talking at once. Maisie is first to approach Mr Mack, 'That was absolutely smashin!, a'll never forget this day. Thanks for lettin us dae it Mr Mack.' Rena at his other side, 'That's a memory a'll take tae America wie me Mr Mack and think aboot when am hame seek.' Martha now thanks him, 'I understand the ceremony much better now Mr Mack, I'll tell my children about it someday.' Lil links arms with Mr Mack, 'See Mack, a told ye they wid appreciate it, they'll see ye in a different light now.'

Mack back to his old glum self, 'Dinnae think it changes onythin, ye'll still only get ten meenits for a smoke' and leaves quickly.

'That was grand, a fair enjoyed it, a got tae be the Braw Lass at last Jean', says Cora.

'So ye did Cora, it fair tane me back, oo yist tae dae it every year. A've never got tae be the Braw Lass, still maybe next year.'

Lil taking charge again 'Well girls, by the time oo get this place back tae rights it'll be hame time, lets get to it'. As they put the tables back in place Maisie says 'What a super day its' been, hasn't it Rena', 'Oh aye it's been smashin'.

Then turning to Jessie 'When div oo get oor Gala Day fund Jessie?', 'It's usually Thursday hen', 'Oh that's all right, on Thursday a'll be rich.'

As they take off their scoogies and pick up their bags and bits and pieces Maisie tells everybody 'Am gettin fair excited for the Gala Day.'

Jean not wanting anybody to forget her new possession says in a loud voice 'A wonder what'll be on the television set the night.' 'Probably an awfae nice ornament' Lil tells everybody, and they all laugh, even Jean.

As the hooter sounds they all link arms and Lil shouts 'Lets go girls' and Jean reminds them 'Mind yer photaes the morn'. They exit singing 'Pomper-ee-om pom pom pom Braw Braw Lads'.

The End

Mixing of the Roses. Braw Lads' Gathering, 1953. Braw Lad Lawrie Grant, Braw Lass, Margaret Finlay.

Old Town Cross

This ceremony commemorates the marriage of James IV of Scotland to Margaret Tudor (descendant of Royal Houses of York and Lancaster) in 1503 which became known as the marriage of The Thistle and The Rose, and led directly to the Union of the Crowns in 1603.

Her dowry – the Lands of Ettrick Forest – of which Galashiels was part, was received by her representatives in the traditional ceremony of sod and stone (sasine) at or near the site of the present Old Town Cross. Witnesses of the ceremony were Walter Scott of Buccleuch, David Hoppringill of Galashiels and William Hoppringill of Torwoodlee.

Today the Braw Lads and Lasses re-enact this ceremony in traditional style. By mingling of red and white roses of York and Lancaster, and placing them in a base of thistles. Sod and Stone from Torwoodlee Tower are also offered and placed by the Braw Lass at the base of the original shaft of the Old Town Cross.

The Laird of Gala or his representatives then present the President of the Gathering and the officials of the Braw Lads' Gathering Executive Council with the Charter, granted in 1599, creating Galashiels as a Burgh of Barony. The Laird then receives the acknowledgement of the people of Gala.